OLIVES AND BARBED WIRE

Impressions of Palestine and Israel

by
Sue Beardon,
Patricia Cockrell
and David Mitchell

Designed by Joan Curtis
Printed by PMM Group, Harrogate. Tel: 01423810111
All photos by the authors
Published by Zaytoon Press
ISBN 978-1-907188-53-4

Sue Beardon, Patricia Cockrell and David Mitchell worked for Quaker
Peace and Social Witness as ecumenical accompaniers on the World
Council of Churches' Ecumenical Accompaniment Programme in
Palestine and Israel (EAPPI). The views contained herein are personal
to them and do not necessarily reflect those of their former employer
(QPSW) or the WCC.

5 shekels = £1 (approximately) at time of visit
4 dunums = 1 acre (approximately)

Contents

Introduction

Sue, Patricia and David were based in placements in the north of the West Bank, in Yanoun, Tulkarem and Jayyous. Jayyous and Tulkarem are both located on the separation barrier, and Yanoun is surrounded by outposts of one of the Israeli settlements called Itamar. According to the United Nations, there are around 144 such settlements in the West Bank, accommodating around 400,000 settlers. These settlements are considered illegal under international humanitarian law. The Fourth Geneva Convention, Article 49, paragraph 6 states "the occupying power shall not deport or transfer parts of its own civilian population into the territory it occupies". United Nations resolution 242 in 1967 affirmed that Israel's presence in the West Bank constituted a hostile occupation, and as such the stipulations of the Geneva Convention apply. This has also been confirmed by the International Court of Justice. Many of the outposts are also illegal under Israeli law.

The Palestinian territories of the West Bank and Gaza have been occupied by Israel since the six-day war in 1967. Occupied Palestinian Territories are known as oPT, and this is the abbreviation we use in this book.

The structure, part 8m high concrete wall and part alarmed fence with barbed wire, built by the Israeli government on Palestinian land, is known by the Israelis as the *security fence* and by the Palestinians as the *apartheid wall*. We have chosen to use the neutral term the *separation barrier*. We have also chosen to speak of the *Israeli army* rather than the *Israeli Defence Force*, and *settlements* rather than *colonies*.

This selection of our newsletters home is intended to give a sense of what life is like for ordinary people under a military occupation. We also include newsletters we wrote from other places we visited in both the West Bank and in Israel.

Opposite: "Ahlan wa sahlan" (welcome!)

A Country of Contrasts

Sue Beardon is from Sheffield where she lives with her husband Michael, who supported her wholeheartedly. (But he hopes not to go through it again!) She is retired from twin careers as organisational consultant and walking guide. Being an outdoor enthusiast she was happy to serve time in the beautiful rural north of the West Bank. As a signatory to Jews for Justice for Palestinians, she was keen to broaden her experience of the conflict and play a part in redressing injustice. Sue has a daughter and two grandchildren.

Is there a better way to start the day than sitting by the taboun watching Najiha form the dough into elastic pancakes, moving them deftly from hand to hand and placing them onto the smouldering coals? She offers me one fresh, hot and delicious piece of the bread to take home and share with my colleagues for breakfast with sheep's cheese and apricot jam. Next door there are three old ladies – I say old, at least two of them are probably younger than me. Quite often one of them will approach wielding a small bottle of roasted almonds. This morning I relent and buy one. 20 shekels, about twice the price I would ever pay in England. These ladies do not know about the market economy, supply and demand. I visit Najiha again for an Arabic lesson. I probably learn some Arabic, but mostly I get to know Najiha, who I like more and more. She is such a strong and bright woman, a force of nature.

Today Rafik and I visit Askar Camp, a refugee camp set up after 1948. We have a meeting at the Women's School Society. Apparently, the man I met on a bus last week from Askar lives only two streets away and the women very kindly give him a call for me. He comes straight round, and gives us a tour around the camp. Buildings are so close together in some places that open windows touch each other across the street. Children follow us in droves shouting "Wayne Rooney", "What is your name?" and sometimes slightly ruder things which I am sure they don't know the meaning of. There are over-crowded schools for the thousands of children who live here. Our guide Tayseer was born in the camp 45 years ago and has never left. Public workers are on strike at the moment, so rubbish is piling up in the streets, schools closed, health at risk. Tayseer is most concerned. At his house, where about 40 members of his family live on three floors, his brother also joins us. He lived in Australia for 20 years and has an Australian wife, Gillian, who also joins us. They came to live here 22 years ago, when they had 4 children in tow and another on the way. She speaks fluent Arabic and works for UNWRA in charge of clinics throughout the north of the West Bank. Palestine Monitor carried an article about her entitled From Sydney to Askar Camp. Yesterday I could not have had a more contrasting experience, joining a group called Shat-Ha for a delightful very early morning hike north of Ramallah. After three hours of hiking we stopped for a wonderful breakfast under pine trees on a hill opposite an Israeli settlement. Someone made a fire and boiled water for tea. The company was funny and interesting, mainly teachers from Bir Zeit University. They were fascinated that we came from Yanoun and plan to visit us and the people there soon. I felt sad that I could hike there but not around Yanoun, which is, if anything, even more beautiful, but surrounded by settlement no-go areas.

Above: a child plays in the narrow streets of Askar refugee camp, Nablus.

Left: the village taboun where bread is baked each morning.

A Piece of Heaven in Hell

I visited the most inspiring place in Palestine. Near Bethlehem is The Tent of Nations. The brothers Daoud and Daher run it on land bought by their grandfather in 1916. Here they run summer camps for children from refugee camps and local villages. They plant trees. Internationals come to support and work here. It is part of the network for Working on Organic Farms. There are 100 acres of land tucked in between a block of Israeli settlements known

as Gush Etzion. When their grandfather came here he dug caves for the family to live in. International visitors can still stay in one of the caves.

In 1991 the nightmare started. Israel claimed the land was state land and wanted to evict them. Fortunately, the brothers had all the papers going back through the various occupations of Palestine, from the Ottoman period, the British Mandate and the Jordanian period. They went to court to prove the land was theirs. The court wanted maps, they made maps. The court wanted aerial photos, they had them taken at great expense. The court wanted testimonies from 40 people in the nearby village – they brought the people to the court, who were subsequently made to wait hours in the sun until hearing the session was

The peace stone at the Tent of Nations near Bethlehem.

Sue planting an olive tree in land belonging to the Tent of Nations, the home of the Nasser brothers. Internationals come to support them in fighting to retain their land.

postponed. They have spent nearly 20 years fighting this case. Whatever it costs, they keep fighting on. They lost 250 of their trees to road building for the Israeli settlements. Settlers have come to break into the land, trying to establish caravans and new outposts there. More and more internationals started to gather to protest and send the settlers away. Settlers came with guns whilst one of the children's summer schools was running. Daher said, "Put down your guns and come in to drink tea," but the settlers broke in with their guns instead. The road to their property has been blocked with large boulders to prevent them bringing produce in and out. He took a bulldozer to clear the road and was arrested. There have been demolition orders on their tents, fences, even their caves! The court came to the land with settlers and the brothers showed all their papers. The settlers showed a tiny piece of paper with a verse from the Old Testament. They have been offered money, but still they will not go.

For the last 13 years the Tent of Nations has become a centre for peace, understanding and bridging between people. Many Israelis have come and helped. Even a woman from the settlement came, and was shocked at what she heard and saw. She brought her husband and others who helped build composting toilets there. These people have since left the settlement for Jerusalem. Jewish children came to play with Palestinian children. Soldiers came in a jeep to check on what was happening, but left when they saw all was peaceful. One time an army jeep got stuck on the road block they had created, and Palestinian children came down to help lift the jeep free. Daher said "When you make a problem, I try to make good, because I want to make change".

Sue Beardon

A Rural Paradise?

The village of Upper Yanoun and its olive groves, home to Sue and her team and all the internationals who have provided protective presence for the inhabitants.

Our first night in Yanoun settlers came into the village after dark and stole fruit from 18 olive trees. The following morning the alarm was raised as a large group of people descended from the hill top. They were hikers. And why not? This is a beautiful place. Limestone hills surround a lush valley, and olive trees climb each hillside. But no locals hike here. Shepherds keep their sheep on the lower slopes and olive trees higher up are abandoned. And these hikers carry guns. They come from Israel with maps that do not show any villages here.

I am reminded that in Sheffield, where I live, people fought in the 1930s for access to land to ramble and enjoy the countryside. Here people do not even have access to land which is theirs to make their living. For they are ringed by hostile settlers – of the most militant and violent kind. Most recently a mosque was torched. To his credit, a liberal rabbi from near Bethlehem personally bought new Qurans for the rebuilt mosque. But only a few days ago settlers came down to threaten the mosque again.

With the olive harvest starting people are gearing up for attacks. We attended a rally in nearby Burin with speakers from the Palestinian Authority, to try to co-ordinate the olive harvest in all the local villages. There is safety in numbers.

Another village, Madama, used to have plentiful water from a spring above the village, but twice now settlers have destroyed pipes bringing the water to the well, and now, like so many other places, people pay to have water brought in tankers by Israeli water companies.

At Rashed the mayor's house there is a poster of an olive tree with the slogan "I will not leave". People have left the village, but many are determined to stay. It is their land and losing it means losing Palestine. Our neighbour Kamal jokes that they have given up trying to travel to Jerusalem because of the difficulty of getting permits. "There are checkpoints even to get into heaven," he says.

The following morning I walked down to Lower Yanoun to meet the head man there, Adnan, who is at home, as it is Friday, taking care of his three children. Minna Tullah, meaning gift from God, is a charming curly headed four year old and Ali is a nine month old terror. The older boy is studying. Adnan is a chemical engineer working for the Palestinian Authority in Nablus. He says our presence here is helpful. "Look" he says, "In much larger villages than this, settlers attack, torch houses and mosques, but here things are much quieter, even though there are only eight families here – why? Because the settlers see internationals."

Whilst in Jerusalem we hear that one local village had a children's playground demolished by the Israeli army after children threw stones, and the village will get the bill. The day I left Yanoun it had been raining and a rainbow spread from the top of the hill where the settlements are down into the valley and the people were beginning to pick olives. Two peoples, who seem destined to live in fear and hatred of each other are for one moment linked by its light.

Adnan, the deputy mayor of Yanoun, and engineer working for the Palestinian Authority, with his youngest son Ali.

Sue Beardon

An Audience with Father Ibrahim Nairouz

Father Ibrahim is the minister for the Anglican churches in Nablus. He speaks of the wisdom of Solomon and the two mothers who claim the one son. Solomon suggests that the child be cut in half, and the true mother, preferring to give up her child than to see him cruelly butchered, bows to the false mother. "Palestine is small like that baby," says Father Ibrahim. But who, I wonder, is the true mother who will give up the child in order to save its life? "Just read the bible," he says. "Take out the limits put on our thinking by Zionism and find a comprehensive solution." Father Ibrahim quotes liberally from the bible. As he warms to his theme, he lays out his compelling vision with eloquence.

For him there can only be a "one state" solution. "We have five major problems" he says, "Settlements, Borders, Water, Refugees and Jerusalem – with one state, all these problems disappear. Settlers become neighbours, borders are settled, water is for everyone, refugees can live where they like and Jerusalem will be for all the people." But it is easy to say, more difficult to achieve.

He thinks a two state solution will not work in the long term. All through his exposition, he stresses the word "harmony", harmony with each other, harmony with nature, harmony with the way of God. "You can move the course of a river by force," he says, "but sooner or later your force will weaken and the river will return." There are no natural borders within the whole land of Palestine and Israel – "If you go against nature and against God, you cannot sustain it. What people have to learn here," he says, "is the beauty of diversity. When you use more colours, the picture is more beautiful." We ask him if Christians are leaving Palestine. He is at pains to stress that the idea that Islam is driving Christians away is completely false. "Christians in Arab countries are Arabs; they have an Arab mentality, a mentality they share with Moslem neighbours. We live in harmony with Islam. It is the occupation which is driving people away. The occupation has resulted in

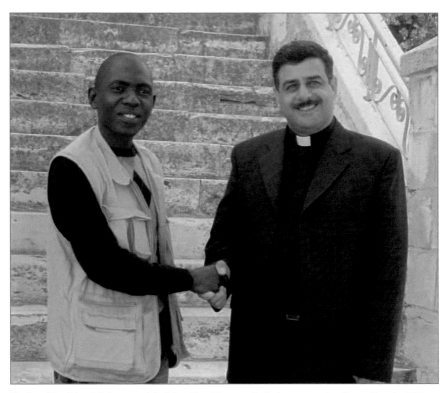

Father Ibrahim Nairouz with Mandla, Ecumenical Accompanier from South Africa, after spelling out his vision of a one state solution for Palestine and Israel.

massive unemployment, lack of opportunity, lack of safety and security." He also points out that although pilgrims from all religions are free to go to their holy places, Arab Christians are not so free. They cannot go to the Jordan River, to Nazareth, to Jerusalem, and even going to Bethlehem is difficult because the journey takes so much longer now, due to the wall. Last Easter he obtained permission to go for one week to Jerusalem, but because it coincided with the Jewish festival of Pesach, all borders were closed and he was unable to use his permit. Two elderly women from his community wanted to make pilgrimage to Nazareth. He worked hard to get permission for them. He was only given permission for one day. He argued for two days, and eventually the Israelis relented. But when it came to it, these were two consecutive days, but without the night in between. It became impossible to go. The headlines in Israeli newspapers said that permission had been granted for Christians to go to Nazareth, but the priest refused to take them.

Sue Beardon

"They only come here to demolish our village"

From Yanoun you used to be able to walk over the mountain for about 15 minutes to reach Khirbet Tana and from there an easy step to the Jordan Valley. Khirbet is Arabic for a tiny hamlet, and indeed Tana is tiny. It's where shepherds take their flocks for the winter. There are three springs there. They can grow fodder for their sheep. And it is idyllic. The people had built a little school for their 20 children to attend whilst they live in this remote place for the winter. They built structures to house the sheep during lambing, to protect the small, vulnerable lambs from the cold and rain. They live in caves, but also had erected tents for their growing families.

On Wednesday morning we received a message that Israeli soldiers had ransacked the place, demolishing tents, animal shelters and the school. Because there is an illegal Israeli settlement on the hill between us and Tana

Khirbet Tana in the Jordan Valley after Israeli bulldozers destroyed the village school.

A Khirbet Tana man stands beside his demolished WC - an obvious security risk!

it takes us over an hour, driving around to the Nablus road, past Huwarra check-point, through Beit Furik and down another 8 kilometres of unmade dirt road. The scene when we arrive is so depressing. The headmaster stands beside the ruins of the school, next to the 300 year old mosque, which, thank heavens, remains intact. An old man sits with his head in his hands. People are in shock, even though, we discover, this is the third time in two years this has happened. Last January the school was demolished and it took them four months to rebuild. The children were due to start school next month, and now this. They will now have to do the 8k dirt road there and back to Beit Furik every day. The army inform the people that this is a military area, needed for training. News to them, as they have used this land for over 100 years and have the Turkish papers from Ottoman days to prove it. One man says, "We never see the army here unless it is to demolish our houses!" He is probably in his late 60s and he says his grandfather was killed by a Turkish soldier during that occupation. *Plus ça change.* During the winter 180 people live here with their 7000 sheep. There is nowhere else they can live with so many animals. The soldiers did their work between 6 and 7 in the morning. It is now midday and already people have re-erected shelters and started bringing in what supplies they can to rebuild. The grim determination and stalwart nature of these people is inspiring. We sit and drink tea with one family of three generations. Beside us is one destroyed tent, together with the ruins of their corrugated iron toilet. We ask if there will be help from the Palestinian Authority. One man says, "We are waiting for the PA, just like we are waiting for the rain." They laugh, it hasn't rained properly for almost 8 months.

Sue Beardon

Till We Have Built Jerusalem

Anywhere else in the world it would be a source of joy and celebration to be in such a diverse place. On the Via Dolorosa a parade of Christians carrying a large wooden cross passes two Israeli soldiers leaning on a wall. A waiter shows an Italian couple to a table where two Jewish tourists are already sitting, saying "In Jerusalem we should all be together."

Yet here diversity is unwelcome. Above the souq we stand on the roof overlooking the Dome of the Rock and the Al Aqsa Mosque. Around us flutter Israeli flags, a sign of the many settlements established above Palestinian families. Yesterday one such family, clinging to one remaining room of their house, finally had their furniture thrown out on the street.

At the Western Wall of what was the temple mount, orthodox Jews gather to pray. The viewing plaza is filled with celebrating Jews from around the world. Israeli soldiers look on from one corner, relaxing, their guns piled up. As we leave the Jewish quarter there is a clear demarcation where the street cleaning stops, despite the fact that all Jerusalemites pay rates and

Israelis and Palestinians demonstrate together every Friday in Sheikh Jarrah against the occupation and the evictions of Palestinians from their East Jerusalem homes.

taxes. Back along the Via Dolorosa we pass under a house, with a huge menorah and Israeli flag, bought with American money for Ariel Sharon, although he has never lived there.

Away from the old city there are hills and deep valleys, and views to the Dead Sea and the desert. In one of the valleys lies Silwan. Three days ago two children were run over by a settler. He was seen veering into them deliberately. At the police station he denied he had been near Silwan, but he had been caught on camera. Since then children have been throwing stones at buses and cars, and many arrests have been made. Mosa, a member of the community, had his 10 year old son taken away for questioning. He was kept for three days. One of Israel's Knesset members, Michael ben Ari had said at a press conference in the morning that he would kill all the children in Silwan. Avigdor Lieberman, the foreign minister, said that he would have them all arrested – he's a little more moderate!

In Silwan local people protest against the use of archaeology to justify the Israeli occupation.

Silwan, like Sheikh Jarrah, is an area where houses are regularly demolished. Archaeological work is to be carried out in the valley, which is supposed to be where King David walked. Well, where didn't he walk! But these archaeologists are no respecters of a thorough, scientific approach. The skeletons of Muslims are discarded in order to find the archaeological remains that fit the programme.

We were driven out to Ma'ale Adomim, the huge settlement between Jerusalem and Jericho. In a desert the entrance to the suburb is green and ancient olive trees grow, uprooted from parts of the West Bank. The settlement is huge and the houses out of keeping with the surroundings. The settlers here are not the militant religious kind, simply economic settlers, offered lovely houses at knock down prices.

The road we are travelling on between Jericho and Jerusalem does not go where it used to, in a direct line, because now the 8 metre high wall with wire on top cuts right across it. A gas station and shops that used to do a thriving trade now stand in desultory fashion on a road to nowhere.

Sue Beardon

Demolitions in the Jordan Valley

Fasayel in the Jordan Valley – a bedouin village constantly at risk of demolition.

We received a phone call from a contact in the Jordan Valley that the Israeli army were demolishing a Bedouin village near Jiftlik called Abu Alajaj. The Israeli Army came in 20 jeeps and 2 bulldozers around 6 in the morning and bulldozed three sheep sheds and one living unit housing a family of 11 members. Three people, trying to get the animals out of the shed before the demolition, were arrested. Most of the sheep escaped; however, the villagers were still pulling wounded lambs from the remains of the sheds when the team arrived. We were told that 200 lambs were in the sheds and that some may still be stuck under the residue. The villagers were still looking for the sheep that managed to escape before the shed fell over them.

The village's crime is that they are 25 metres from vineyards of illegal Israeli settlement, Massu'a – and the settlers want to take over all the land from the settlement to the road on the other side of the village. Sadie Adnan is the mother of the family that had their house bulldozed. She has a husband and 9 children. She told us that the soldiers said that they are there to demolish their house and commanded them to get outside. Neighbours tried to help them carry out their belongings out before the house was bulldozed. They were beaten and arrested. The electricity was cut and several of their water barrels were also run over.

Her family has lived here for many years; all her 9 children were born here. "I will stay here, I will die here," she said, and added that they will immediately start to rebuild their units and stay with neighbours in the meantime. Around 150 people live in this village and altogether they own around 10,000 sheep. The mayor of Jiftlik said "The Palestinians who live here have no documentation of their ownership of the land. The land belongs to Jiftlik. All the people in this community belong to the same family, the Idaes family. The family is originally from Hebron, but moved here in 1979 as it is not possible to live in Hebron with 10,000 sheep." Pointing at the vineyard only a few meters away, the mayor said, "before 1980 we were on good terms with the settlers living in Massu'a settlement, we were good neighbours. However, with the new generation of settlers everything has changed – now they are not friendly anymore, they want to take our land in order to expand their settlement. They took this land only 7 years ago." He further explained that not many settlers are actually living in the settlement. "It is just that they want our land as if to prepare for more Israelis to come and live here," he said. The Israelis claim that this is their land and that the villagers have built their units without permission. "In this village the imam is not calling out for prayers for fear that the Israeli Army will destroy their mosque," he said. And the next day, this is exactly what happened in a neighbouring community of Khirbet Yarza. When we arrived men were praying in what was left of their small mosque, just a carpet and prayer mats spread out between the mangled piles of stone and iron work. People have been living here for generations, one man tells us. But as life becomes less sustainable people move away. Eleven families live there now, compared to fifty ten years ago.

In Khirbet Yarza Israeli bulldozers destroyed the village mosque. Men continue to pray amongst the rubble.

Sue Beardon

Ukuleles for Peace

Paul Moore runs a ukulele orchestra for children from Palestinian and Jewish families. The children and their parents all meet in each other's houses for rehearsals in the towns of At Tira and Hod Hasharon, one a Palestinian town, one Jewish. Paul's group is called Ukuleles for Peace and it's been going for about 6 years. The young people in it are extremely talented. I had the privilege of attending rehearsals of both the younger and the older groups.

I arrived finally in Karmiel, close to where Paul lives. Recently a right wing group there has been trying to prevent Arabs from settling in the town, because they see Karmiel as key to what they call the Judaising of Galilee. Paul met me there and drove me up to his village high in the West Galilee Mountains, a place called Harashim. There he lives with his wife Dafna, son Alon and 7 cats in a caravan called *The Last Homely House*. He is an ex-hippy from England who came to work on a kibbutz in the 70s and never left. As well as running the ukulele bands, he plays in a jazz band and also performs as a one man band. He is an avid collector of junk and his caravan is crammed to the gunwales with incredible finds – old mannequins, a half strung harp, washboards, grotesque dolls, dried plants and feathers.

The Last Homely House – *Paul Moore's home in the West Galilee Mountains.*

Left: Israeli Jewish and Palestinian
young people play ukuleles and drums.
Above: Paul Moore tunes up.

Everyone is very welcoming, especially the cats. And he offers to put some new strings on my ukulele, which I brought along on the off chance. He did his stint in the Israeli army, and he is adamant that all immigrants to Israel should do this, "…otherwise they cannot really get the picture of what life in this country is all about," he says. He served on the Lebanese border, and had hilarious tales to tell about what he got up to as the platoon joker. His wife Dafna says that she is a Zionist, in that all other peoples have a state, so she thinks the Jews should too. But she does not think this means there should be injustice to Palestinians and she firmly believes in a two state solution.

On the way to visit the children in At Tira we drive down the toll road that goes down the centre of Israel. At one point we pass the town of Tulkarem, which is on the other side of the wall in the West Bank, and there is the wall itself, banked up, with trees and plants to disguise it. I ask Paul and Dafna if they notice it any more, "I'm ashamed to say we don't," Paul admits. In At Tira we sit under a date palm eating the dates directly from the tree and chatting with both Jewish and Palestinian parents. One of the Jewish fathers asks us about our work in the West Bank. When we tell him about the settlers and their vandalism and threatening behaviour, he asks who we report this to. "Why don't you report to the police – these people are criminals," he says. For many Israeli people it is incomprehensible that this should be allowed to go on.

Tulkarem

Patricia Cockrell spent a year in Moscow following graduation and then taught Russian in Exeter for 25 years before being appointed to represent Quakers in Russia, where she worked with international Friends to establish Friends House Moscow.

Preparations for her service in the Middle East involved meetings, trainings, seminars and a great deal of reading. She learnt enough Arabic to get by and tried to learn some Hebrew.

Patricia has two children, four grandchildren, a devoted cat and a long-suffering husband who has made it possible for her to follow the Quaker advice to *live adventurously*, and to whom her part in this publication is dedicated.

On Friday, after several days of training and meetings in Jerusalem, we took the long hot bus ride through vast vistas to Tulkarem. We had had excellent sessions on the history of the Holy Land, the cultures, water issues, permits, guns and international humanitarian law. We had met with peace activists from all sides and also with the UN, who told us what a brilliant job Ecumenical Accompaniers are doing, especially in the villages and at the agricultural gates where there are no other international observers. Jerusalem was fine but it was good to take root in our placement.

In due course it will be hard to say goodbye to the smiling children, the taxi drivers, the old men in the street cafes, and to the baker, who invariably pops in an extra bun, the refugee camp doctor, the pharmacist with his coffee pot, our local contacts, our Arabic teachers and Osama.

There are no street signs. We told our consulates that we live down a bit from Osama's shop and across the road. Next door is a pile of rubble, the result of an Israeli helicopter gunship attack in 2002, but this does not pinpoint us: our pile of rubble is not unique.

We have a small garden flat with room outside for a table and chairs, a washing line and the barbecue which Marcos and I bought for 20 shekels. Marcos is a young lawyer from Portugal and Johan is a researcher at the Peace Institute in Norway. Sara, from Canada, tries to keep us in order. Marcos and I make good use of the colourful ingredients we find in the market, and we love to hear the muezzin's call to prayer as we fan the charcoals and prepare the dressing with local Limpopo-coloured olive oil.

We take turns to monitor the gates which armed soldiers open for a short while mornings and evenings, so that farmers with permits can access their own land, land from which they were separated when the Israeli government built the 'security fence' in 2002; and twice a week at 4am we monitor the checkpoint at Tayba which allows the 3,000 or so people with permits to access low-paid work in Israel. Besides these duties, our tasks include encouraging women's and youth groups in the villages and in the refugee camp which has been home for about 20,000 people since 1948, and offering protective presence during the olive harvest, especially in the villages which are vulnerable to settler violence. We keep in touch with university students, the prisoners' club and Palestinian and Israeli peace groups, and we are called to house demolitions, incursions of settlers or soldiers and nonviolent demonstrations. Oh yes, and we write reports of human rights violations or other incidents, and log our activities, plus any interesting developments or opportunities, every evening.

Tulkarem is on the green line, the internationally recognised 1949 armistice line following what the Israelis call the *War of Independence*, and the Palestinians, because they lost so many people and so much land, and because 750,000 were forced to flee from their ancestral villages, many of which have since been demolished, call the *Nakba*, the disaster.

Farmers queue at the agricultural gate to get to their land which is on the other side of the separation barrier.

23

Patricia Cockrell

Villages

At a meeting in Nablus last week with B'Tselem, the Israeli Information Centre for Human Rights, the Tulkarem team was asked to take on another five Palestinian villages. These are all near to settlements and all have reported problems including incursions by the Israeli army or settlers or both.

Our wonderful taxi driver/interpreter took us to Kifl Harez. How to start making contact with the people here so that we can get an idea of the issues? What about an ice cream?

The shopkeeper on the main square told us that about 200 settlers accompanied by soldiers had come to the village recently demanding access to the mosque in front of his shop: they claimed that two Jews were buried there. They made a lot of noise shouting and firing guns. Nobody was hurt but a woman sitting in her doorway pointed to the bullet holes in her house. What was the outcome? 'We let them to come and pray. We have no choice. We have two other mosques.' Stars of David have been spray-painted on the mosque and on other walls in this ancient village. The little crowd around us shrugged, smiled and thanked us for coming. They said we were the first internationals to visit the village.

The mayors of Immatin and Falatin said that settlers occasionally come into the villages at night to torch the trees and the cars. At Funduk, Yosef told us that the farmers are often attacked when they pick olives. By calling on friends and family they man-

Helping to pick olives.

24

Johan and Marcos at the youth centre project, Kufr al-Labad.

aged to bring in the harvest within the two days of their permit. But will they get a permit to prune their trees this year?

In Harez the shopkeeper has lost 15 dunums of land to settlement building. Was compensation offered? 'Of course not. They build on my land and if I complain, they will close the gate.' Yes, we saw the hated yellow gate which can be locked at any time making it impossible for cars to enter or leave the village. 'You can go and see the bulldozers. They are working every day.'

It would not be safe for our Palestinian taxi to be on this road right under the Israeli army watchtower. So we walked along the road then struck off into the rocky hillside, and there they are – bulldozers and other heavy plant, busy, noisy, dusty. Mahmoud's family have ownership papers going back to Ottoman times. Now it would be dangerous for him to approach the few olive trees that remain between the settlement and the new road. We offered to come and help with the harvest but he remained sceptical. 'What you can do? You have no guns.'

Nevertheless we did pick olives for two hot and dusty days with Ibrahim's family when they asked for our protection in Ramin. They lost trees when a settlement road was built through their land, and they are vulnerable to attack as they harvest the remaining olives. Some settlers stopped to watch us, and an Israeli personnel carrier disgorged six fully armed soldiers who walked wordlessly past us on their way up the hill. 'Without you,' said Ibrahim, 'much trou-

Mahmoud showing Johan the settlement built on his land.

25

Patricia Cockrell

Shufa

Schoolgirls and a herd of sheep on the main road in Upper Shufa.

Shufa village is in two parts: Upper Shufa on the hilltop, and Lower Shufa in the valley below. The two were linked by a steep road of 800m or so. In 2001 the Israeli government closed this road at the bottom with concrete blocks and a yellow gate; the top was also made impassable, and the rest was adopted and incorporated into the settlement road system. It was resurfaced in such a way that cars can sweep by at some speed but there is no room for pedestrians; the donkey and cart is banned, as are all cars with green or white registration plates, ie Palestinian. The villages have been separated, and Upper Shufa is more or less isolated. There is another route out of the village but this is through a checkpoint which is sometimes closed, and the distance travelled to reach Lower Shufa is 25 km. Although there is an element of danger (the safe thing to do is to step off the road into the shallow ditch when a car comes), and people are occasionally challenged by settlers or armed Israeli soldiers, we are encouraged to walk to Upper Shufa to maintain the right of ordinary people to use this 500 year-old recently updated road. Settlement building continues here: you can see the activity from the road, and pile-driving is heard all day every day.

Jamal is headmaster of a school in the valley but he lives with his wife and children in Upper Shufa. It used to be a simple 15-minute journey each day to get to work. He now has to ride his donkey down the hill, and then walk through the concrete blocks and around the gate to reach his car. He tethers the donkey to a tree and then drives to school. If there's shopping to be done in Tulkarem, the donkey does the carrying and Jamal and his wife both walk home, leaving their car at the bottom of the hill.

The 1,300 souls of Upper Shufa depend to a large extent on the olive (our women's group meetings are suspended because everyone is out picking). How do they get the harvest to the presses? By donkey, though there is a lorry that does the long journey once or twice a season.

The top of the road is really only fit for a goat. It is quite a test for a fairly fit 67 year-old woman, so how on earth did Noor manage? Well, it was decided that she would spend the last few days of her pregnancy in Tulkarem so as to be near the hospital. It would have been possible for the ambulance to come the long way round and through the checkpoint but there could be delays. Scores of women have given birth at checkpoints because they are given a three-day permit only, and of course babies have minds of their own. With no professional help, where there are complications there have been fatalities.

As we left Upper Shufa yesterday we were overtaken by a young man on a donkey. The wisest of us all, the donkey finds his own way down the rocky hillside, eschewing the road.

Palestinian vehicles are blocked from using the road to Upper Shufa.

Patricia Cockrell

Hebron

Hebron is horrid. Israeli settlers and soldiers live in the heart of the city together with the 40,000 Palestinians. The 2,000 Israeli soldiers are there not to keep the peace but to guard the 500 settlers. In 1929 67 members of the Jewish community were killed during a Palestinian riot, and in 1994 Dr Baruch Goldstein shot dead 29 men and boys as they were praying in the Ibrahimi mosque. Food aid is delivered to the impoverished Palestinian population by the Red Cross, and several international organisations maintain a presence here, so tense is the atmosphere in Hebron and the surrounding villages.

Shuhada Street, once a prosperous shopping area with stalls and coffee houses, is now closed to Palestinians, and all the shops are shut. Even so, there is a checkpoint across the road manned by seriously bored Israeli soldiers. On Saturdays about 20 settlers, protected by an equal number of heavily armed soldiers, exercise their

Deserted souq in the centre of Hebron. Inset, soldiers guard Israeli settlers.

right to walk through the old city and the souq. Most Palestinians prefer to keep out of the way, and many of the colourful rug, jewellery, embroidery, sweet and other shops are shut. A young woman holding a baby was too scared to cross the square where the settlers had paused with their armed guard. The soldiers were polite to her but still she hung back, trembling and whimpering. I wanted to suggest that she might feel safe if I went first, but my tongue could only manage 'come with me' in Arabic, which sounded a bit peremptory, so I added 'please'. She hesitated but then ran after me and disappeared down one of the narrow passages.

Israeli soldiers keep watch on young Palestinians playing football in the street.

Even though most of them have ownership documents going back to the Ottoman Empire, the villagers in the South Hebron Hills are vulnerable to house demolition, and movement restrictions hinder grazing. All the inhabitants of Susiya were evicted in 1986 when the area was declared to be a national park. They moved into caves nearby but these too were made uninhabitable by the army. They are now living in tents which of course have demolition orders.

The fruit farmers of Beit Ummar asked for our protective presence while they prepare their land. When the rains come, they want to plant 500 trees to replace the ones destroyed by settlers in the last two years. It is dangerous work because of armed settler attacks. At 11am the two EAs and the four other internationals were arrested by the Israeli army. What was the charge? That they were in a closed military area. I worked with Musa, the organiser of this project, for several hours, compiling the list of names and passport numbers, writing the incident report, finding telephone numbers on the internet, and making phone calls. Rabbis for Human Rights gave us the name of an Israeli lawyer who eventually got them released by demanding to see the documents proving that this is a closed military area. Of course I kept in touch with our line manager in Jerusalem who wanted to know why I had not been arrested too. 'Well,' I told her, 'I was in a car crash this morning and was somewhat delayed.' *Allah bahibek* (God loves you),' said everyone as I walked away from the wrecked car. 'God has preserved you for important work. *Ilhamdilla!*'

Patricia Cockrell

Bethlehem

Patricia standing by the 4th Century door of the Church of the Nativity in Bethlehem.

Greetings from Bethlehem! A glimpse of Christmas at last – stars are strung across the streets and nativity scenes light up. In Manger Square this morning I bent down to go through the tiny door of the Church of the Nativity. Constantine's mother Helena built this church in 326 on the spot where she believed the manger had stood. The church was rebuilt in 529 but the 44 limestone columns are the original ones, according to the Russian guide, and you can still see the original mosaic floor. I had a quick look round because I was due to meet the Bethlehem-based EAs at the Coptic liturgy in an incense-filled cave under the road. This is one of the few denominations they had not yet visited.

After a bite of lunch at the flat, we went to the Friday demonstration at Umm Salamone. Settlement building continues around Bethlehem, and the separation barrier, which is still being built, contrary to international law, has deviated more than 17km from the green line. The wall is right in the city, and the convent at the top of our road has been cut off. A neighbour, after negotiating with the Israeli army, was permitted to give the nuns an exit across his land beside the wall. The nuns and their supporters (nobody else is allowed near) walk here every day, partly to maintain their access, but also to pray for an end to the occupation .This evening three of us braved the armed Israeli soldier at the end of the path, and joined the nine people saying the rosary while strolling up and down between untidy rolls of barbed wire. It was very quiet – unlike the demonstration earlier.

We had brought our earplugs, and Terry gave us an onion each and a dry cloth. As soon as you see tear gas or hear someone shout 'GAS', you stamp on the onion and then hold the dry cloth to your face and breathe in the onion fumes. Avoid water – it makes it harder to breathe. No tear gas was used today because it would have blown back towards the 20 or so armed

Welcome to Bethlehem!

Israeli soldiers in Umm Salamone facing demonstrators against the building of the wall.

Israeli soldiers. They used sound bombs instead. Terrifying! One's instinct is to run and hide, but we were warned not to run because soldiers will often shoot at people running away from an incident. Were we a threatening mob of hundreds? There were about 15 Palestinians and 12 internationals including 5 young Israelis, plus a very brave grandmother in hijab and long black gown, who walked past the soldiers carrying a Palestinian flag. This is Suzan whose husband was shot by a soldier and whose son is in prison for 27 years, leaving her in charge of his three small daughters. The young Israelis led the singing and dancing. They also made impassioned speeches in Hebrew and in English about nonviolence and the corrupting influence of apartheid. The soldiers appeared to be listening. Who knows? Perhaps they will join the growing number of former soldiers prepared to speak out against the occupation. *Inshallah!*

Meanwhile, happy Christmas preparations! You have the snow, the holly and the ivy; I have the donkey, the star and Manger Square. I also have the wall, guns, barbed wire and soldiers shouting at me to remove my shoes: I too had to go through the checkpoint in socks.

Jerusalem

Olive trees in the Garden of Gethsemane.

At last I am cracking the mysteries of the Old City, a place of noise and colour, narrow lanes and tall buildings, busy souqs, dark staircases leading heaven knows where and ethnic quarters. I ask directions of the young Jews because they are so ready to smile at lost grandmothers, and I superimpose these images onto the faces of the gruff soldiers barking orders at checkpoints. They are the same young people transformed by uniforms and guns.

Will the taxi driver waiting at Jaffa Gate take me to the Israel Museum? 'Is now traffic jam. *Trib* (there's no p in Arabic) ten minutes, could take hour. What you want to see?' 'The Dead Sea scrolls…' 'I take you to Dead Sea, no *broblem*.' 'No, the scrolls…' 'OK, I take you to Qumran.' Heavens! Do I look like a rich tourist? But suddenly he suggests Chagall. Yes, the Chagall windows are on my list of things to find during my days off in Jerusalem. So here I stand beside the Citadel where Pilate lived, chatting with an Arabic taxi driver about Chagall.

We agree a price and Ahmed drives me to Ein Karem where Chagall's windows depicting the 12 Tribes of Israel are displayed in the huge hospital. Can this be right? I am directed to a staircase which says DELIVERY ROOM. I don't want to disturb the young mothers and grandmothers with their newborns in plastic trolleys, so I accost a doctor who directs me to a huge dovecote on a flat roof. Wonderful!

I have my *Lonely Planet* of course but I also like to bob in and out of organised tours: here's a French group at the Orthodox Church on the Mount of Olives, there's a Russian group at the monastery; and a German guide at the Garden of Gethsemane says that Jesus would have seen and touched some of these olive trees.

'*Batricia*! You want I take you home?' It's Ahmed waiting for his customers. 'I come in half an hour.' Perfect. I've walked miles today. He joins me 20 minutes later at the little café with the best view of Jerusalem in the

Israeli soldiers passing Mary's Tomb, East Jerusalem.

evening light – there is a *broblem*, but his cousin will take me home. 'Don't worry! Meet me at Mary's Tomb, ten minutes.'

There are pilgrims, tourists, a few priests and nuns at Mary's Tomb when a column of about 250 armed soldiers walks through. I snatch a couple of photos including some astonished onlookers, but Ahmed grabs me and steers me into a car. 'Photos of soldiers not good. Could be questions. Better go quickly. Is my cousin.'

The cousin is the very image of Arab brigandry. 'I saw you in Silwan.' Er, I can't quite gather my thoughts. Silwan, where Jesus healed the blind man, is a deprived Arab area of Jerusalem with demolition orders on many of the houses. Our bus was stoned but we got out anyway to show that we meant no harm. 'Yes, EAs were there. What happened to the children who were run over?' 'They are home from hospital. They are in house arrest.' 'And the settler who was filmed aiming his car at them?' 'Nothing.' The cousin is called Jamal. 'Call me if you need me.' I will.

When possible Patricia joined the Women in Black at their weekly demonstration in West Jerusalem, see **Neve Shalom.**

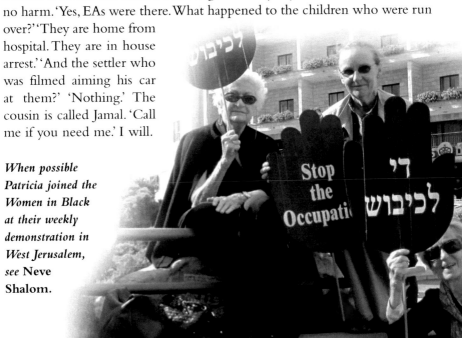

Patricia Cockrell

Neve Shalom

Together with the other women I am being abused and shouted at by passers-by on Perez Square in the centre of Jerusalem, though there are a few waves and smiles of support. *Women in Black* have demonstrated here against their government's military occupation of Palestinian territories and the blockade of Gaza every Friday lunchtime since 1988. The women refuse to apply for permission to stand on their own street wearing whatever they like, ie black. They are scornful of the policemen sent "for our protection, ha!", but I am quite glad of their presence.

What is the future here? "There is no future. We were full of hope and enthusiasm once, but we have created a monster. There will be war but I will not be here, thank God. I am 89," says Aviva. Maya speaks of the problem with the media: a liberal government cannot come to power because of the oft-repeated fear of threats to security. "The Arabs are not seen as real people, but as dangerous garbage." Anne invites me to visit Neve Shalom, a pioneering village in Israel.

There's no public transport. I rang Ahmed – would he drive us to Neve Shalom from Jerusalem? Yes, and the price seemed reasonable, so I gathered a carload of interested EAs, and Anne, one of the founders of the village in the 1970s, showed us around.

Anne Le Meignen – one of the Women in Black and a founder member of Neve Shalom.

The village is run by the people who live there, Arab and Jew side by side fostering tolerance and understanding. Arab and Jewish children from neighbouring villages attend the bilingual and multi-cultural school, and there is now a waiting list. "All the festivals are celebrated," said Anne, with a twinkle, "Jewish, Muslim and Christian. Oh yes, we have a lot of holidays, but then that's what life is about, especially when you are a child. We enjoy each other's cultures and traditions while nurturing each child's identity." What

Marcos in the Doumia, Neve Shalom.

happens to the children when they leave here and move on to the more nor-mal sectarian secondary schools? "Our children are special children. They will never lose that respect for the other. It is very encouraging that so many parents want this education for their children."

Families can of course worship where they choose but there is no mosque, synagogue or church in Neve Shalom. The spiritual centre of the village is the Doumia or House of Silence, the white dome for reflection and meditation, which was opened in 1980 by Anne in memory of Bruno Hussar, the co-founder of the village. In 2006 the Meeting, Prayer and Study House was opened for cross-cultural encounters and training courses pro-moting the vision of a humane, egalitarian and just society.

Ahmed did not object to our staying for four rather than the agreed two hours, in fact after some persuasion he joined the tour and the simple lunch, even though he does not really feel at home in Israel. We gave him an extra 100 shekels in recognition of the fares he had not taken that afternoon, and hoped he had enjoyed the visit. "*Batricia*," he said, 'you good woman. You all good *beoble*, you and your friends. Always must ring me when you in Jerusalem." Well, I've kept his number.

Patricia Cockrell

The Kibbutz

New buildings at Kibbutz Metzer with our host Dov Avital (inset).

Dov Avital invited us to his kibbutz. Kibbutz Metzer is still run by a system of integrated committees with an elected overall chairman, on the principle of need, ie a family with three or four children will have more living space than a single person or a couple of pensioners.

Metzer is next to Qalqilia but on the other side of the wall, the separation barrier. Land belonging to farmers in Qalqilia, which they can of course no longer reach, was given by the Israeli government to the founders of the kibbutz, who had asked for coastal land: the Argentinian Jewish Marxist pioneers were sailors and fishermen, not farmers. Aged over eighty now, they freely admit that, knowing nothing about making a living from the land, they would not have survived the early years without the support of their Arab neighbours.

When they discovered that the land they had settled was not ownerless, they offered compensation to the farmers of Qalqilia, but Arab policy has almost invariably been, and still is, not to accept compensation because this would seem to legitimise the confiscation of their land by turning theft into commerce. They would prefer to give the land to people who need it and will make good use of it. Dov and the management committee of the kibbutz occasionally meet with a delegation from Qalqilia, but this is difficult to arrange as Qalqilia is completely surrounded by the 8 m concrete wall, and Dov, who could get through the checkpoint with his Israeli ID, says he will never again set foot in the West Bank until the end of the occupation.

The kibbutz is named in honour of their other Arab neighbour, Meizer, which by chance finds itself on the Israeli side of the wall. Relationships between these two communities are much easier to maintain in spite of their differences: one is religious, the other atheist; one is a patriarchal society, the other lefty-liberal. "But still we decided to explore cooperation rather than fighting," Dov said, "if it doesn't work, we can fight later, but why waste resources?"

To their mutual benefit they have cooperated on various schemes including an electricity supply, irrigation and projects for the recycling of water. "Why can't they see it?" Dov asks. "Water is our biggest problem, not whether we are Jewish or not. Still the Americans and the EU cannot see that recycled water does not have to be potable. For them a scheme is not worth looking at if all you are doing is watering your crops, but for us this is life – for all of us."

"The Israeli government does not like us because we have found the solution. The solution is simple. There is no synagogue on the kibbutz because it is easy to say, 'God is on my side. God gave me the land'; nor do we want to spend time on looking for the burial place of the servant of the wife of the Prophet Mohammed, said to be hereabouts. Far harder and more productive, and ultimately more satisfying, especially if we can do it together, is to produce food, to look after each other and to give all our children a safe environment."

Bananas growing on the kibbutz.

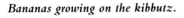

First Impressions

David Mitchell is a 66 year old Scot from Oban in the West Highlands. A family man with two grown up children, he and Sheila, his wife, have visited Palestine before in a private capacity and, like others, have become addicted. After qualifying as a marine engineer, David spent 20 years as a Human Resources Manager, covering the UK, Europe and the Middle East. A family bookselling business occupied the last 20 years until retirement. David and Sheila are both active members of The Church of Scotland.

It's four thirty in the morning on Monday 4th October, and the sound drifting through my window is one of the most evocative, sensual and for many millions, most meaningful sounds in the world. It is the sound of competing mosques all over the city of Jerusalem calling the faithful to prayer and for me it marks the start of a three month spell as an Ecumenical Accompanier (EA) with the World Council of Churches Ecumenical Accompaniment Programme in Palestine and Israel (EAPPI). After all the long learning and training processes, the adventure has begun!

The next time I hear a similar sound is three days later in the small agricultural village of three thousand souls, called Jayyous, in the north west of the West Bank. This time the call to prayer at 4.30am performs the additional function of awakening the villagers to work at the start of the olive harvest, the farmers' busiest time of the year and two of the hardest months in their calendar.

But for these farmers there are very particular additional difficulties in their farming lives unlike any other. You see they have been separated from their land by a barbed wire barrier. Armed Israeli soldiers unlock the gates in the barrier for a short period at around 6am, at midday and again at 4.45pm so that the farmers with permits can access their land and get home again. These are the lucky 20%! The other 80% are denied access to their land altogether! The barrier referred to is of course the infamous Israeli security fence but more aptly named the separation barrier, which was seemingly arbitrarily built across Palestinian land, without the consent of the owners or any compensation paid. The International Court of Justice gave an Advisory Opinion in 2004 that the barrier is illegal under international law and should be removed from Palestinian land and the owners compensated.

Several years later and it's still there, standing like a grotesque monument to man's inhumanity to man, while the occupying forces of the Israeli army, under the guise of 'security', continue to make a mockery of international humanitarian law. The expression, 'one law for the rich and one law for the poor,' could, if changed to 'one law for the powerful and one for the powerless' just about cover it, but the scandal is that we are complicit by continuing to allow our politicians to place political expediency above the application of just laws.

But somehow, life here goes on. Like all farmers everywhere, their attachment to family land is absolute and seems only to strengthen with every injustice heaped upon them. The autumn rains came today, giving the olives hanging heavily on the branches a helpful wash before collection. We EAs were with the farmers when the rains came, helping pick the harvest, and a jolly time was had by all. We danced about in the rain until all were drenched through, then we retreated to 'Chateau Jayyous' (our residence and anything but a castle) while they carried on harvesting. For a few hours walls and barriers were forgotten.

And we remember that its only when the night is darkest that we see the stars most clearly.

Above: Israeli soldiers on duty at Jayyous North Gate.

Right: EAPPI negotiating with Israeli soldiers on behalf of farmers.

39

David Mitchell

Jayyous in Focus

The view of Jayyous from the west.

Jayyous enjoys wonderful panoramic views across the separation barrier to the lands and water wells which belong to the village, and beyond into Israel. On a clear day, we can see the Mediterranean Sea, but the villagers have no permits to travel there. None of the village children and very few of the adults, if any, have been to the sea. Living in Oban, with our feet practically in the water, I find that unthinkable, but it is the least of their worries.

The village is surrounded by olive trees (zeitun). Most of the best land is on the other side of the separation barrier. This is where amazing fruit and vegetables are grown, including many I have never seen before (even Tesco doesn't have them!). Why was the separation barrier built to exclude the farmers from their most productive land and their wells? The official Israeli view for this is 'for security reasons', but one cannot help being drawn to the conclusion that the real policy is to squeeze out the Palestinians and steal their land and water. If you fear your neighbour, you build a fence around your own land, not half way through his!

The village has piped water from a neighbouring village (Azzun) since it cannot access its own wells on the other side of the barrier, but this water is expensive and so they rely on the rainy season to fill the water cisterns.

Sometimes they have to arrange for a water tanker to fill up their cisterns, but this is expensive. Electricity is also available but quite unreliable. I prefer not to ask about sewage treatment but everyone seems to remain healthy!

Other than agriculture there is little employment in the village, and nothing much for young people to do other than play volleyball. Jayyous has one of the best volleyball teams in the oPt, and the village boasts an impressive indoor volleyball court. Despite the lack of activities, I am not aware of social disorder or vandalism. Of course there is no alcohol here, although I hear that one of the village shops has applied for permission to sell beer! The scandal!!

Of course family life is very strong, as is community life, and contrary to some of the negative publicity which its detractors put about, I feel that the Muslim faith encourages, if not demands, high moral standards. The local people are extremely generous and hospitable. A walk in the village is often punctuated by invitations to join families for tea or coffee, which are most welcome in the heat, and the best meal in town is to be had at the olive press where bread is soaked in the new, green oil. The taste is stunning, so vibrant and light!

I am very proud to say that there is a direct connection between Jayyous and the Church of Scotland in that the Guild sponsors the crèche here, and a great boon it is to the young mothers of the village. In addition to the direct help it provides, it is so important that they know that someone out there cares for them.

In a world which has let them down very badly over the years and seems to allow their oppressors a free hand, the people of Jayyous and of all of the oPt need all the help they can get.

The Jayyous team.

Orwellian Nightmares Live on

It was the look on the elderly woman's face that told the story more eloquently than any words could manage. Her house in Jayyous had been forcibly entered at 2am on Monday morning (25/10/2010) by armed Israeli soldiers complete with dogs. Hiding their faces with balaclavas to retain anonymity, they arrested her son Wajdi (27) without explanation, and trashed many of her belongings. Her daughter Hind, who was also present in the house at the time of the break-in, told us that up to fifty soldiers had taken part. "My mother, who is quite frail as you can see, was also injured by the soldiers pushing her," she said, "and required hospital treatment before being discharged." The soldiers had stayed from 2am to 5am, keeping the whole household up, and had systematically searched room after room leaving a trail of destruction and despair, including vandalising Wajdi's computer.

Wajdi's room after an early morning raid by the Israeli army.

The scene of our meeting was the open court yard of their modest home in the heart of the small agricultural village of Jayyous, in the Qalqilia District of the West Bank, and my two Ecumenical Accompanier colleagues and I were re-living with the family the nightmare happenings of that morning. The Israeli army had entered the village with stealth and had forced their way in before the family were even aware of their presence. At the same time, another two families in the village were

Wajdi Bayda's gate was forced open during the raid on his house.

suffering a similar experience, in an operation which is mirrored across the occupied Palestinian territories somewhere virtually every week.

No word of explanation was offered according to Hind, and they have no idea where Wajdi will be held, or when they will see him again. Experiences of this kind lead the villagers to believe that he will be held in an Israeli prison (contrary to International Humanitarian Law), perhaps without charge and consequently without recourse to a defence. This is *legal* under the military law which Israel applies to the occupied Palestinian territories but not to its own citizens. It should be understood that time spent in prison for Palestinians is not at all unusual and a substantial proportion of the male population has been locked up at some time, usually for unspecified *threats to security* which are never explained and never prosecuted. According to the *Palestine Monitor* there are currently in excess of seven thousand Palestinian prisoners being held in seventeen Israeli jails and investigation centres scattered widely across Israel. This number does not include those in Israeli holding centres in the Palestinian territories. Even if permitted, it is often extremely difficult for families to visit their loved ones because of problems with travel and with the expense involved.

PS…This story took a twist in mid November when Wajdi, who was still locked up and had not been charged with any offence, was offered his freedom on paying a fine of 3000 shekels (about £600), which his family could not afford. In early December he was given an unconditional release date of 19th December.

David Mitchell

So Near and Yet So Far

I had planned to meet an old family acquaintance from Bethlehem a few nights ago. I had sent her an email arranging to meet outside the Damascus Gate of the Old City of Jerusalem, and I settled down to await her arrival. What arrived first was an email asking if I had forgotten that as a Bethlehem resident, she is not permitted to enter Jerusalem. This young person, who has just earned her Masters Degree in International Law from The London School of Economics and who was back at her permanent residence for a short holiday with her parents before returning to her studies in London, was not permitted to travel the few kilometers from her home to the Palestinian capital.

Like hundreds of thousands of her compatriots, she is a victim of the Israeli military occupation and its illegal policy of denying freedom of movement to Palestinians in their own country. This is a fundamental right under the Fourth Geneva Convention which Israel is signed up to. However the daily challenge for large numbers of workers and other civilians is to navigate the closures which restrict their movements: checkpoints, road closures, concrete blocks, earth mounds and farm gates which allow farmers to have limited access to their own land. The issuing of permits by the Israeli authorities to allow travel across these internal man made obstacles seems to be quite arbitrary; it is also ageist and racist. The permit system disrupts family life, education, worship, agriculture, commerce and the provision of health services; it is in breach of the International Declaration of Human Rights.

The shopkeeper half way down the Jericho Road wasn't happy either. The separation barrier (a wall in this case), which was started in 2002 ostensibly as a 'security fence' to protect the Israelis but which is now generally suspected as being used to demarcate a new border, was built straight across the road. It stopped through traffic overnight, killing his business and enforcing on him a 45 minute journey to see his son's family, who had lived next door before the barrier separated them. It was of little comfort to him that the wall had subsequently been heavily graffitied and bore the evidence of a sympathetic Scottish hand, but I thought it cool.

Evidence of a sympathetic Scottish hand on the separation barrier.

I was speaking to a Palestinian about these and all the other restrictions placed upon them by the military occupation and commenting that I could see no pattern or logic to them. "Ah," he said, "you've spotted that. That's the whole point. It is totally random, unconnected to security or anything else for that matter, and designed to frustrate us; nothing else."

Welcome to the West Bank.

David Mitchell

Processing People

Palestinian workers queue at the Qalqilia checkpoint.

One of the Jayyous EA team's less desirable weekly duties is to monitor activities at the workers' checkpoint at Qalqilia, a large town of about 50,000 people and a 30 minute taxi ride from Jayyous. The function of this checkpoint, a gate in the separation barrier manned by armed Israeli security personnel, is to allow workers from the oPT to access jobs in Israel. Only those who have been granted the appropriate permits by the Israeli authorities will be allowed through. Permits have acquired a huge importance for the Israelis as a means of controlling the movement of the Palestinian population, and for the Palestinians they are an essential path to earning a living under occupation, as unemployment is a major problem in the West Bank.

This EA duty is unpopular for two reasons: first because the monitoring team must wake at 2.45am to reach the gate for its opening at 4am and stay until 7am, and second, because the work involves witnessing the degrading spectacle of between three and four thousand workers being lined up, identified by five different parameters and if all are correct, being allowed to progress to their work perhaps one or two hours later. If they are unlucky, and this could involve as little as a slightly torn permit or an unrecognised palm print (imagine a labourer being able to guarantee his palm print on an unreliable computer day after day), then the permit is confiscated and a new one has to be applied for from the Israeli authorities. This can take days or even weeks and meantime the worker earns nothing and he could lose his job because of the delay.

There was a new variation on the frustration theme this morning: one angry worker was sent back because he had taken a litre of Palestinian milk with him, no doubt to drink in midday temperatures well in excess of 30 degrees. He caught our attention when he reappeared at the turnstile which he had entered probably an hour before, and hurled the offending milk over our heads before starting the queuing process all over again. Not even the lunch boxes are unaffected! Palestinians are not generally allowed to take certain foods into Israel, although Israeli settlers are allowed to take anything, even though their farms are right next to Palestinian ones. Indeed many of their farms are claimed by the Palestinians to have been acquired via some doubtful legal processes, if not by force.

This may seem a fairly trivial matter until you consider that Palestine had a large cash crop agriculture industry, mainly from small family enterprises, which fed neighbouring towns and the less fruitful adjoining areas and countries. Now, due to the restrictions of the occupation they are not allowed to transport their goods across checkpoints into Israel, so cutting off their biggest markets. Added to that, Israel will not import Palestinian goods, and so their agriculture industry has been brought to its knees. Meantime, West Bank shops are well supplied with Israeli produce. As a counter to this, the Palestinian Authority has trained hundreds of volunteers to help Palestinians to recognise illegal settler produce and to find Palestinian alternatives.

What can we do to help from so far away? We can do what the Palestinians are doing. When shopping, we can be careful not to buy produce which comes from illegal Israeli settlements (ie. all Israeli settlements in the oPT), and we can encourage the corner shop and the supermarket not to stock them.

Power to the people!!!

David Mitchell on duty at Qalqilia North checkpoint at 4.30am.

Settlers

The terms *settlers* and *settlements* take me back to the films of my child-hood, the cowboy adventures with intrepid families in wagon trains fighting their way westwards in search of a better life in the wild west of the USA. We view the ethics of that movement rather differently now, but from a perspective of British Empire and all that, it seemed not so bad then.

The terms are a bit more confusing now when used in the context of the oPT. Six years ago, Professor Greg Filo and Mike Berry of the Media Studies Group at Glasgow University produced a study, later published as a book entitled *Bad News from Israel*, which showed confusion among British students as to what the terms mean when applied to the oPT. To quote one reviewer, "Only 10 percent of the groups of British students interviewed in 2001 and 2002 knew that it was Israel that had occupied the Palestinian ter-ritories. Some even thought that the Palestinians were the occupiers. Many saw the conflict as some sort of border dispute between two countries fight-ing over land."

The Palestinian people in the villages of the oPT have no such doubts! Their ability to survive as farmers is irrevocably tied up with the olive har-vest as a subsistence crop, but the harvest also brings vandalism, theft, arson and physical assaults from some adjacent Israeli settlements and their occu-piers. These settlements spring up on Palestinian land, usually on hilltops with just a few mobile homes to start with, populated by ideologically driv-en Israelis. They quickly develop into townships, then fully fledged and fully serviced towns. The Israeli Government claims not to approve but is quick to supply electricity and water to the settlements and to give them the pro-tection of the Israeli army. The settlers claim surrounding land by the use of force (Israel allows them to carry arms, while the Palestinians cannot) and to deny local farmers access to their own land. Olive trees are cut down, burnt or stolen by settlers, and attacks on Palestinian families harvesting their olives are documented every year.

All of these settlements on Palestinian land are illegal under internation-al law (Article 49, Fourth Geneva Convention), and, incredibly, the interna-tional community does nothing to enforce it, and so the settlers' expansion-ism and lawlessness go unchecked. From a Palestinian point of view this must stop as a precondition for peace talks. Put simply, stop illegally taking land for settlements and we can talk peace. The Israeli position is this: we insist on

Olive tree on fire in the village of Burin after settlers from Yitzhar attacked.

continuing to take land and on building illegal settlements while talking peace. Meanwhile the country dies and the custodians of international humanitarian law, the international community of which the UK is a part, stand on the sidelines doing nothing effective.

I'm sorry about this rant, but I am afraid the so-called international community really is not implementing the UN Resolutions or international humanitarian laws which they have signed up to do.

And the one question I have not addressed is the claimed justification for this settler behaviour. Wait for it!! It is their land because they are God's chosen people and He gave them it. And Palestinians who have farmed the land for generations must give it back!

Send for the Cavalry!

David Mitchell

Psalms Ch.18 v 29.

You really never know what's round the next corner, do you? Last week I was in the small village of Al Ma'asara to observe the weekly demonstration against the encroachment of the Israeli separation barrier which takes place every Friday, and has done for several years. This village, along with several others just south of Bethlehem, has lost valuable agricultural land (reputed to be 850 acres from Al Ma'asara alone) to the wall.

The demonstration started off with a social gathering in a vacant house, with locals and internationals mixing with a film crew from a Palestinian television station. When the time came to start, a few of the people up front waved smallish Palestinian flags as we set off walking up the narrow main road, a fairly motley crew of about thirty, of all ages and nationalities. At the crossroads at the far end of the village things changed! Out of the blue, we were charged by three Israeli army vehicles which appeared directly in front, and soldiers confronted us with machine guns at the ready. They formed a cordon across the road and stopped us dead in our tracks. Still, all was calm among the Palestinian group, who did not move. I should clarify that EAs do not take part in demonstrations, we just observe from a safe distance, so my two colleagues and I remained back from the front line. That didn't help when the Israeli soldiers started throwing sound bombs (properly called concussion grenades). The front line simply stepped aside, and the

Tear gas is used against demonstrators in Al Ma'asara (see opposite).
Spent sound grenade (inset)

grenades rolled on to our 'safe' place at the back! These devices make a very loud and frightening noise when they explode but by and large do no harm unless they are very close, so the trick is not to be very close!

When this failed to disperse the demonstrators, things got more serious. We were charged again but this time the soldiers seemed determined to catch someone to arrest. They fired tear gas over our heads and chased the stragglers. Folks, I can tell you I was not one of the stragglers. It is quite amazing just how fast you can run when there is a soldier with a gun in hot pursuit. We ran through back gardens, jumped garden walls and fences, and generally acted like children having been caught stealing apples. And during this time my more experienced colleague said she heard sounds like rubber bullet shots or live rounds being fired. No one was hurt however, and no one was caught!

On reflection (and after I had caught my breath), the ridiculous nature of the whole unnecessary affair struck home. On the one side, not much more than a Sunday afternoon stroll became the object of violence. On the other, unnecessary armed interference in a harmless exercise could have caused death. And who won? The TV crew got the dramatic footage they wanted presented to them on a plate by the Israeli army, and the protesters got the publicity they wanted.

So what did the Israelis get for their trouble? Answers on a postcard please, except there is no postal service in Jayyous!

And the reference at the top of the piece? Maybe that's how I cleared those fences and walls?

David Mitchell

The Road Less Travelled

Our host, Nomika Zion said, "In the months before the Gaza war they were coming in at a rate of sixty a day." The Israeli housewife and peace campaigner had invited Ecumenical Accompaniers to visit her at her home in Sderot and she was referring to 'qassam' rockets being fired at her town from Gaza, only two kilometres away.

Over the years since the first rockets were fired in 2001, 19 Israelis have been killed, mainly in and around Sderot, and many more have been injured. Rockets began falling at a greater rate, she explained, after the incursion into Gaza by the Israeli military in November 2008. This resulted in the deaths of ten Gazans and it broke a pre-existing ceasefire which had been effective in gaining support for Hamas, the ruling political force in Gaza. After the cease-fire, rocket attacks from Gaza diminished significantly; after the Israeli incursion, the rocket fire resumed with a vengeance. Nomika had written to Prime Minister Olmert of Israel and President Abbas of Palestine, pleading for a restoration of the ceasefire but to no avail. When the war started – operation Cast Lead, December 2008 – and Gaza was invaded by the Israeli army, Nomika told us that half of Sderot emptied. People were terrified and terrible damage was done to both populations and to the soldiers because, as she put it, "war pollutes the soul". She was anxious for her family, her friends and neighbours, for the soldiers and for the Gazans who, she maintained, were not her enemies. A low point came when a letter arrived from a fourteen year-old Gazan girl who pleaded, "Help us, we are human too!"

Nomika Zion from Sderot – one of the founders of **The Other Voice.**

Nomica sent an article to a German newspaper *Not in My Name and Not for My Security* which was translated into several languages and published in *Time* magazine and on several websites. While labelled by many as the enemy of Israel, she has had an avalanche of support from many people including Israeli citizens. So

A playground caterpillar doubles as a rocket shelter in Sderot.

that those Israelis who share her views can find solidarity, she started a movement called *Other Voice* whose principles include dialogue, reciprocity, empathy, mutual respect, non-violence and non-partisan local activism. "Both sides are victims," she said, "caught up in an endless round of violence. We don't talk of peace any more in Israel. Politicians use the word, but they don't mean it. We seem to believe we have to fight, and it's senseless".

Among other activities currently being planned are a continuation of the campaign to end the siege of Gaza, joint seminars with residents of Gaza to facilitate meetings between young people, business people, women's groups, mental health professionals etc., meetings with Israeli residents, outreach projects and the co-creation of a web-site with the Gazans.

It's hard to overestimate the courage of this remarkable lady and her co-workers in *Other Voice*, Eric Yellin and Julia Chaitin, who day by day test their faith in human nature in a very hostile environment, and sacrifice friendships and even sometimes family relationships in the cause of international peace and justice. Indeed, they have chosen "the road less travelled" and a harder one is difficult to imagine. It becomes very clear that on both sides of the Israeli separation barrier there are remarkable and courageous people working for the benefit of all of us and who deserve our encouragement and prayers. *See* www. othervoice.org.